Urban Exploration - Paris The Comprehensive Travel Guide

PA BOOKS

Published by PA BOOKS, 2023.

While every precaution has been taken in the preparation of this book, the publisher assumes no responsibility for errors or omissions, or for damages resulting from the use of the information contained herein.

URBAN EXPLORATION - PARIS THE COMPREHENSIVE TRAVEL GUIDE

First edition. October 29, 2023.

Copyright © 2023 PA BOOKS.

ISBN: 979-8223602934

Written by PA BOOKS.

Also by PA BOOKS

Hogan's Key
Kimberly & the Five Strange Goldfishes
The Enchanted Library
The Misadventures of Pirate Pete
From Wheel To Web: 40 Remarkable Inventions
Once Upon A Sleepy Time
The Global Game - The Evolution Of Football
Strides To Success: A Beginner's Guide to Running
The ChatGPT Handbook
Climate Crossroads
1000 Everyday Life Hacks
Urban Exploration - London The Comprehensive Travel Guide
Urban Exploration - New York The Comprehensive Travel Guide
Urban Exploration - Amsterdam The Comprehensive Travel Guide
Urban Exploration - Barcelona The Comprehensive Travel Guide
Urban Exploration - Dubai The Comprehensive Travel Guide
Urban Exploration - Paris The Comprehensive Travel Guide

Table of Contents

Chapter 1: Introduction to Urban Exploration in Paris

Welcome to the captivating world of urban exploration in the City of Light. Paris, a city renowned for its iconic landmarks, world-class cuisine, and rich history, holds a trove of hidden treasures awaiting your discovery. In this chapter, we embark on a journey to unravel the secrets, delve into the history, and prepare you for the extraordinary experience that is urban exploration in Paris.

A Brief History of Urban Exploration

Urban exploration, often shortened to urbex, is a global phenomenon rooted in the desire to uncover the forgotten, the overlooked, and the hidden within our cities. Paris, with its centuries of history and a surplus of neglected or repurposed spaces, serves as a natural canvas for urban explorers to roam.

Urbex dates back to the 1970s when it first emerged as a subculture in Europe and the United States. Early urban explorers sought to document and explore abandoned industrial facilities, drain systems, and asylums, all while capturing the beauty of decay through photography. The movement has since grown into a worldwide community of adventurers who embrace the thrill of entering off-limits locations.

The roots of urban exploration can be traced back to the catacombs of Paris. The vast network of tunnels and ossuaries beneath the city, known as the Paris Catacombs, was the first documented site to be explored by enthusiasts. Initially, it was visited by a small group of explorers, but as word spread, the catacombs became a symbol of urban exploration.

Today, urbex is not merely an endeavour but an art form. It encompasses a wide array of sites, including abandoned factories, hospitals, schools, and more. Paris, a city steeped in history, provides a particularly rich backdrop for this art.

Safety Tips and Ethical Considerations

Safety is paramount when embarking on an urban exploration adventure in Paris. Remember that you are often entering abandoned or off-limits areas, and unforeseen risks can be part of the allure. Here are some key safety tips and ethical considerations to keep in mind:

1. Always research and plan: Before heading out, thoroughly research the location you intend to explore. Understand its history, potential dangers, and legal implications.

2. Travel with a group: Whenever possible, explore with a group of fellow urban explorers. Not only is it safer, but it can also enhance your experience.

3. Respect private property: Urban exploration should never involve breaking and entering. Always respect "no trespassing" signs and the boundaries of private property.

4. Dress appropriately: Wear suitable clothing, including sturdy shoes, gloves, and protective gear. Bring a first-aid kit and a flashlight to navigate dark spaces.

5. Be discreet: Keep a low profile when entering and exiting locations to avoid drawing unnecessary attention.

6. Leave no trace: Take nothing but photographs, leave nothing but footprints. Avoid leaving any evidence of your presence, and do not vandalize or steal.

7. Abide by the law: Remember that some locations may be legally off-limits. Do your best to adhere to local laws and regulations.

8. Be cautious in the catacombs: If you venture into the Paris Catacombs, be especially vigilant. The tunnels can be labyrinthine, and it's easy to become disoriented. It's advised to have a guide or a detailed map.

9. Respect the environment: Many urban exploration sites are fragile and may contain hazardous materials. Be mindful of the environment and your own safety.

10. Document, don't disturb: Capture the beauty of decay through photography and storytelling. Avoid moving or altering items within locations.

Why Paris Is a Great City for Urban Exploration

Paris, with its intricate tapestry of history and modernity, offers a unique urban exploration experience. Here are the reasons why this city is a treasure trove for those who seek to uncover its hidden gems:

1. Historical Depth

Paris has witnessed centuries of history, wars, revolutions, and cultural shifts. Many abandoned or overlooked sites in the city retain echoes of the past. From Belle Époque theatres to World War II bunkers, Parisian urbex offers a rich historical narrative waiting to be unravelled.

2. Architectural Diversity

The city's architectural diversity is a playground for explorers. You'll encounter a mosaic of styles, from medieval buildings to grand Haussmannian boulevards, and even avant-garde structures. Each tells a different story of Paris's evolution.

3. Underground Mysteries

The Paris Catacombs, a network of subterranean tunnels and ossuaries, are a world unto themselves. Descending into this dark, enigmatic realm, you'll explore a side of Paris rarely seen by the average visitor.

4. Hidden Artistic Gems

Beyond the Louvre and Musée d'Orsay, Paris hides galleries, ateliers, and street art installations in its less-travelled corners. Urban explorers can uncover the works of both renowned and emerging artists in unexpected places.

5. Unconventional Vistas

The Eiffel Tower, Notre-Dame, and Montmartre are iconic Parisian landmarks, but urbex allows you to see these treasures from unconventional angles. You'll discover hidden vantage points and perspectives that few have the privilege to experience.

As you embark on your urban exploration journey through the heart of Paris, keep these historical roots, safety tips, and the city's allure in mind. In the chapters to follow, we'll delve deeper into the neighbourhoods, sites, and stories that make Paris a must-visit destination for urban explorers. Get ready to discover the hidden side of this enchanting city.

Chapter 2: Montmartre: Bohemian Elegance

Unveiling the Bohemian Essence of Montmartre

Welcome to the enchanting neighbourhood of Montmartre, a realm of artistic allure, winding streets, and a rich cultural history that beckons the urban explorer to explore its depths. In this chapter, we will delve into the essence of Montmartre, painting a vivid picture of its artistic heritage, its picturesque streets, hidden artistic havens, and the secrets that lie beneath the iconic Sacré-Cœur Basilica.

The Artistic History of Montmartre

"Montmartre", once a rural village just outside Paris, gained fame in the late 19th and early 20th centuries as a haven for artists, writers, and musicians. This artistic nucleus quickly became known as the heart of Bohemian Paris.

Artists' Retreat: Montmartre was a sanctuary for countless artists, including Henri de Toulouse-Lautrec, Amedeo Modigliani, and Pablo Picasso, who sought inspiration in its cobbled streets, dimly lit cabarets, and vibrant atmosphere. The neighbourhood's liberating spirit allowed these creative souls to experiment and push the boundaries of art.

The Moulin Rouge: Immortalized in the famous painting by Henri de Toulouse-Lautrec, the Moulin Rouge cabaret became a symbol of Montmartre's vibrant nightlife. It still stands today, offering mesmerizing cabaret shows and a nostalgic glimpse into the past.

The Bohemian Way of Life: Montmartre fostered a sense of freedom and nonconformity, attracting writers like Émile Zola, Rainer Maria Rilke, and Suzanne Valadon. The neighbourhood encouraged these individuals to rebel against societal norms and conventions.

A Walk through the Charming Streets

Begin your exploration of Montmartre with a leisurely stroll through its charming streets. Here are some of the must-visit locations that embody the neighbourhood's unique character:

1. Place du Tertre: This bustling square, often referred to as the "Artist's Square," is a hub of creativity. Local artists display their work here, offering you the opportunity to watch them at work and perhaps even commission a portrait or painting.

2. Rue des Saules: A picturesque street lined with historic houses, Rue des Saules encapsulates the essence of old Montmartre. As you walk along its cobblestones, you'll feel like you've stepped back in time.

3. Le Bateau-Lavoir: This artistic residence in Montmartre was once the home to some of the most influential artists of the 20th century. Picasso, Braque, and Gris all lived and worked here, shaping the course of modern art.

4. Lapin Agile: A legendary cabaret, Lapin Agile, known as the "Nimble Rabbit," continues to attract visitors with its intimate ambiance and traditional French chansons. It has been a gathering place for artists and poets for over a century.

5. Moulin de la Galette: This historic windmill-turned-restaurant offers a taste of Montmartre's past. You can savour French cuisine while enjoying the lovely views from its terrace.

6. Montmartre Vineyards: Yes, you read that correctly. Montmartre boasts its very own vineyard, Clos Montmartre, which produces a unique wine served at special events in the neighbourhood.

7. Montmartre Cemetery: While not as famous as Père Lachaise, this cemetery is a serene place for reflection and the final resting place of several notable figures.

Hidden Art Studios and Cafes

Montmartre has a knack for concealing creative nooks and crannies that are often overlooked by tourists. Discover these hidden gems:

1. Atelier de la Lumiaire: Tucked away on Rue des Saules, this charming photo studio is dedicated to preserving the art of collodion wet plate photography, offering a glimpse into the past.

2. Maison Rose: This whimsical, pink-painted restaurant is an ideal place to dine while immersing yourself in Montmartre's artistic history. Picasso is said to have once exchanged paintings for meals here.

3. Halle Saint-Pierre: This arts and culture centre, often overlooked by tourists, showcases an eclectic range of contemporary and outsider art.

4. Le Consulat: A cosy and traditional café, Le Consulat is where artists like Utrillo and Modigliani once gathered. It's the ideal spot for a leisurely coffee or a glass of wine.

5. Musée de Montmartre: Nestled in a charming villa, this museum showcases the artistic heritage of Montmartre and offers beautiful gardens with a view of the city.

Sacré-Cœur Basilica and Its Secrets

The crown jewel of Montmartre is the Sacré-Cœur Basilica, perched on the highest hill in Paris. This architectural masterpiece, completed in 1914, boasts secrets and surprises of its own:

1. The White Dome: The brilliant white dome of Sacré-Cœur is adorned with 300,000 tiles, which exude a radiant luminescence in the sunlight.

The basilica's architectural grandeur and commanding presence are an ode to the city of Paris.

2. Spectacular Views: Ascend the dome's 300 steps, and you'll be rewarded with breath-taking panoramic views of Paris. From here, you can admire iconic landmarks such as the Eiffel Tower, Notre-Dame, and the Arc de Triomphe.

3. The Crypt: Beneath the basilica, a crypt houses a collection of religious art and artefacts, as well as the tomb of the church's founder, Alexandre Legentil. It offers a glimpse into the basilica's history and significance.

4. The Nightly Vigil: Every night, since 1885, a perpetual vigil has been maintained in the basilica to atone for the sins of humanity and to pray for peace. It's a moving and solemn tradition that continues to this day.

5. A Place of Worship and Harmony: Visitors are welcome to attend Mass and witness the basilica's role as a centre of spirituality and community.

Montmartre invites you to step into the world of the great artists who found inspiration here, to wander its charming streets, and to uncover its hidden treasures. This bohemian enclave is more than just a neighbourhood; it's a living canvas, a place where art, history, and culture intersect.

Chapter 3: Le Marais: Timeless Beauty

Discovering the Timeless Beauty of Le Marais

As you venture deeper into the enchanting tapestry of Paris, you'll find the historic district of Le Marais waiting to unfold before you. In this chapter, we invite you to explore the timeless beauty of Le Marais, replete with its rich historical overview, hidden courtyards, hôtels particuliers (private mansions), the vibrant Jewish Quarter, and an array of trendy boutiques and cafes.

Historical Overview of Le Marais

Le Marais, which translates to "The Marsh," is a district that encapsulates the very essence of Paris's historical past. This former marshland was initially drained in the 12th century, giving rise to a neighbourhood that has evolved through the ages.

Medieval Roots: In the Middle Ages, Le Marais was a thriving centre of commerce and industry. This can be seen in the neighbourhood's narrow, winding streets and grand hôtels particuliers, which were often the homes of aristocrats and nobility.

Renaissance Splendour: In the 17th century, Le Marais was home to many royal residences, including the stunning Place des Vosges, the oldest planned square in Paris. The neighbourhood continued to attract the wealthy elite, fostering a climate of opulence and artistic refinement.

The Paris of the Belle Époque: Le Marais was also at the heart of the Belle Époque, a period of great artistic and cultural achievement. It was during this era that many of the district's most iconic buildings, squares, and boutiques were established.

World War II and Revival: Le Marais played a significant role in World War II, as it was a hub of Jewish life and culture. Today, it stands as a testament to resilience and revival, offering a harmonious blend of history and contemporary chic.

Hidden Courtyards and Hôtels Particuliers

Le Marais is a treasure trove of architectural marvels, often hidden behind unassuming facades. The district's courtyards and hôtels particuliers are gems waiting to be discovered:

1. Hôtel de Sens: Dating back to the 15th century, this splendid hôtel particulier was the residence of the Archbishop of Sens. It now houses the Forney Library, a haven for book lovers.

2. Musée Carnavalet: Explore the history of Paris within the walls of this magnificent hôtel particulier. The museum's gardens and salons provide an enchanting backdrop for learning about the city's past.

3. Hôtel de Ville: The Paris City Hall, with its grand courtyard and stunning architecture, stands as a symbol of the district's importance in the heart of Paris.

4. Hôtel de Sully: Hidden behind a discreet entrance, this hôtel particulier boasts a serene garden, offering a peaceful retreat from the city's hustle and bustle.

5. Place des Vosges: A perfect square enclosed by beautiful hôtels particuliers, this place is a delightful spot for a leisurely stroll. The elegant arcades surrounding it are home to art galleries and charming cafés.

6. Le Village Saint-Paul: A secret oasis in the heart of Le Marais, this village-like area features narrow alleyways, antique shops, and delightful boutiques.

Explore the Jewish Quarter

Le Marais is renowned for its thriving Jewish Quarter, a vibrant and historically significant area where culture and tradition intertwine:

1. Rue des Rosiers: This bustling street is the epicentre of the Jewish Quarter. Explore kosher bakeries, falafel stands, and shops that sell everything from Judaica to vintage clothing.

2. Shoah Memorial: This moving and informative memorial pays homage to the memory of the Holocaust and the Jewish victims of World War II.

3. Synagogue de la Roquette: An architectural gem, this synagogue is a testament to the enduring Jewish presence in the neighbourhood.

4. Le Marché des Enfants Rouges: The oldest covered market in Paris, this market offers a rich variety of international cuisine, making it an ideal spot for a culinary adventure.

5. The Jewish Art and History Museum: This museum beautifully illustrates the history, culture, and art of French Jews.

Uncover Trendy Boutiques and Cafes

Le Marais is also known for its thriving contemporary scene. As you explore, you'll find an array of trendy boutiques and cafes that blend old-world charm with modern flair:

1. Concept Stores: Le Marais is home to an array of concept stores that stock everything from high fashion to interior design, making it a fashionista's paradise.

2. Le Peloton Café: A favourite among cyclists and coffee enthusiasts, this café offers a cosy atmosphere and a warm cup of coffee.

3. Merci: A concept store with a charitable twist, Merci boasts a curated selection of fashion, homeware, and accessories.

4. Popincourt: A boutique filled with exquisite handmade leather goods, offering an authentic taste of Parisian craftsmanship.

5. L'Éclair de Génie: Satisfy your sweet tooth with exquisite éclairs in innovative flavours at this delightful patisserie.

6. La Perle: A historic cafe known for its unique ambiance, it's where celebrities and locals mingle. It's the same place where the famous singer Edith Piaf found her beloved Marcel Cerdan, the French boxer.

Le Marais, with its historical grandeur and modern-day allure, offers a blend of old and new that's nothing short of mesmerizing. This district is a living testament to the city's multifaceted past and a thriving hub of culture, art, and creativity that continues to evolve with each passing day.

Chapter 4: Canal Saint-Martin: Hipster Haven

Exploring the Vibrant Charms of Canal Saint-Martin

Canal Saint-Martin, nestled in the heart of Paris, is a dynamic, ever-evolving district that thrives on a unique blend of creativity and history. In this chapter, we invite you to discover the hipster haven that is Canal Saint-Martin. Prepare to witness the transformation of this canal area, uncover captivating street art and graffiti hotspots, explore quirky boutiques and vintage shops, and be enchanted by the picturesque locks and footbridges that make this district a true gem in the city.

The Transformation of the Canal Area

Once an industrial zone, Canal Saint-Martin has undergone a remarkable transformation over the years. It has evolved from a working-class neighbourhood to a thriving hub of art, culture, and community.

The Canal's Origins: Built in the early 19th century under the reign of Napoleon I, the canal was initially conceived to supply the city with fresh water and serve as a means of transport for goods. Today, it offers Parisians and visitors a charming respite from the urban hustle and bustle.

The 21st-Century Renaissance: In recent decades, Canal Saint-Martin has seen a renaissance that has attracted a hip, creative crowd. The area is now dotted with trendy cafes, boutiques, and art spaces, making it a magnet for those seeking an alternative, artistic atmosphere.

Community Vibe: The canal serves as a focal point for the local community. It's a place where residents and visitors alike gather to enjoy picnics, boat rides, and leisurely strolls along the water's edge.

Street Art and Graffiti Hotspots

Canal Saint-Martin is a canvas for street artists and graffiti creators. As you explore, you'll come across vibrant, thought-provoking works that add an extra layer of character to the district:

1. Rue de la Grange aux Belles: This street is a treasure trove of street art, with walls adorned with striking murals, colourful graffiti, and intricate stencils. Keep your camera ready, as the art is ever-changing.

2. Le Mur: Known as "The Wall," this space on Rue Oberkampf serves as an open-air gallery where artists are invited to create their work. Witness the monthly transformation of this space.

3. La Petite Ceinture: The abandoned railway tracks of La Petite Ceinture that once circled Paris have become an intriguing canvas for street artists. This off-the-beaten-path gem is a must-visit for urban art enthusiasts.

4. Rue Denoyez: A narrow, vibrant street filled with eclectic street art and graffiti, Rue Denoyez is a kaleidoscope of colours and creativity. You can even catch artists in action as they work on their latest pieces.

5. Urban Art Galleries: Explore the numerous galleries in the area that focus on street art, such as Galerie Itinerrance, which showcases the works of renowned urban artists.

Quirky Boutiques and Vintage Shops

Canal Saint-Martin is a paradise for shoppers looking for unique and offbeat finds. The district is dotted with quirky boutiques and vintage shops, each with its own charm:

1. Antoine & Lili: This boutique is a burst of colour and creativity, offering a whimsical collection of clothing, accessories, and home décor items. You'll find a range of eclectic and international products here.

2. Kiliwatch Paris: A multi-story concept store that combines vintage clothing with contemporary fashion. It's a treasure trove of unique finds for fashion-forward shoppers.

3. Chez Adèle: This vintage store is a haven for antique lovers. Explore an array of carefully curated items, including furniture, clothing, and accessories from bygone eras.

4. Les Fleurs: A boutique specializing in unique and imaginative floral arrangements. It's the perfect place to pick up a bouquet or admire their artistic floral creations.

5. Artazart Design Bookstore: For book lovers and design aficionados, this bookstore is a paradise. It offers a wide selection of art, design, and photography books, as well as a unique array of stationery and gifts.

The Picturesque Locks and Footbridges

Canal Saint-Martin is adorned with picturesque locks and footbridges, adding to its charm and appeal. These iconic structures are an integral part of the district's identity:

1. Locks of Love: As you stroll along the canal, you'll come across the charming locks that dot the water's path. They serve as both functional

components of the canal's infrastructure and popular spots for romantic gestures.

2. Footbridges of Elegance: Canal Saint-Martin is punctuated with a series of elegant footbridges that allow pedestrians to cross the water. Each footbridge offers a unique perspective and a delightful view of the canal.

3. The Colored Bridge (Pont des Récollets): This footbridge, known for its distinctive blue colour, is a favourite spot for both tourists and locals to capture picturesque photographs of the canal.

4. Pont Saint-Ange: This ornate bridge, named after an angel, is a work of art in itself. Its intricate ironwork and decorative details are a testament to the artistry of 19th-century Paris.

5. Bridge of Double Locks (Pont des Double-Écluses): This lovely bridge boasts two locks and has an air of timeless romance. It's an ideal place to take in the tranquil scenery.

Canal Saint-Martin is a testament to the vibrant, artistic spirit of modern Paris. As you explore the transformed canal area, you'll encounter an eclectic blend of creativity, history, and community, making it a must-visit destination for those seeking a hipster haven in the heart of the city.

Chapter 5: Père Lachaise Cemetery: Haunting Beauty

Exploring the Haunting Beauty of Père Lachaise Cemetery

Père Lachaise Cemetery, a place of tranquil repose and haunting beauty, beckons you to wander its leafy avenues, where the stories of the famous, the lesser-known, and the legends are eternally inscribed in stone. In this chapter, we'll embark on a journey through this historic cemetery, paying tribute to its famous residents, unearthing the remarkable but often overlooked graves, delving into tales of love and loss, and immersing ourselves in the eerie beauty that envelops this hallowed ground.

The Famous Residents of Père Lachaise

Père Lachaise Cemetery is a who's who of the great, the artistic, and the influential, with mausoleums and gravesites that draw admirers from around the world.

1. Jim Morrison: The iconic lead singer of The Doors found his final resting place at Père Lachaise. His simple, unassuming grave is a pilgrimage site for fans, adorned with graffiti and tributes.

2. Oscar Wilde: The Irish playwright and poet, known for his wit and literary genius, has a unique tomb adorned with lipstick kisses, evidence of his enduring popularity.

3. Édith Piaf: The "Little Sparrow" of France, the legendary chanteuse, rests in eternal song. Her grave is a testament to her enduring appeal.

4. Frédéric Chopin: The composer's heart is said to be encased in a pillar at Warsaw's Holy Cross Church, while his body lies in Père Lachaise. Visit his grave to pay homage to his musical brilliance.

5. Marcel Proust: The acclaimed author of "In Search of Lost Time" found his final inspiration within Père Lachaise, where he continues to captivate visitors.

6. Maria Callas: The opera diva, known for her unparalleled voice and tumultuous life, rests beneath a simple yet elegant tombstone.

7. Eugène Delacroix: The Romantic painter is celebrated with a monument featuring a bronze relief of his artwork. It's a must-see for art aficionados.

8. Gertrude Stein and Alice B. Toklas: The artistic and literary couple share a tombstone adorned with heartfelt tributes from admirers.

9. Victor Noir: The unconventional tomb of this journalist and political activist features a life-sized statue rumoured to have fertility-enhancing properties. It's an unusual sight amid the solemn surroundings.

Lesser-Known, But Remarkable Graves

While Père Lachaise is famous for its notable residents, the cemetery also holds countless stories of remarkable individuals whose graves deserve recognition:

1. Théodore Géricault: The influential Romantic painter behind "The Raft of the Medusa" is interred in a quiet corner, often overlooked by visitors.

2. Guillaume Apollinaire: The renowned poet and art critic's grave is adorned with a sleek, modernist monument.

3. Isadora Duncan: The pioneering American dancer, known for her innovative approach to dance, has a beautifully sculpted monument that captures her grace.

4. Félix Nadar: The pioneer of aerial photography and portrait photography has a unique grave featuring a photograph of himself.

5. Balzac's Monument: Honour the literary giant Honoré de Balzac with a distinctive monument erected by his devoted readers.

6. Louis Braille: Pay tribute to the inventor of the Braille system for the visually impaired, whose grave features a raised Braille inscription.

7. Camille Pissarro: The Impressionist painter's grave is marked with a serene sculpture that reflects his artistic spirit.

8. Maria Malibran: The 19th-century operatic sensation's tomb features a poignant sculpture of a mourning woman.

9. Héloïse and Abélard: The ill-fated lovers, Héloïse and Abélard, have a touching monument that commemorates their tragic yet enduring romance.

Stories of Love, Loss, and Legends

Père Lachaise is steeped in tales of love and loss, as well as legends of ghostly apparitions:

1. The Legend of Oscar Wilde: It is said that the statue atop Wilde's grave, known as "The Angel of Death," occasionally weeps black tears. Some claim this is the result of a curse placed on the tomb.

2. The Ghost of Jim Morrison: Urban legends persist about the ghostly presence of Jim Morrison, who is said to wander the cemetery and nearby streets.

3. The Phantom Drummer: Legend has it that a phantom drummer is heard near the grave of Frédéric Chopin. Some visitors claim to have heard his music in the night.

4. The Cross of Light: During World War II, a mysterious luminous cross appeared in the sky over Père Lachaise, believed by many to be a divine sign.

5. The Tale of Eloise and Abelard: The star-crossed lovers' story continues to captivate visitors. You can visit their graves and reflect on their enduring love story.

The Eerie Beauty of This Historic Cemetery

Père Lachaise Cemetery possesses a haunting and ethereal beauty that transcends the realm of the living. The allure of its winding pathways, shadowy crypts, and solemn atmosphere is undeniable. As you explore, take note of these hauntingly beautiful features:

1. Ancient Trees: Towering cypress trees and ancient oaks cast eerie shadows over the tombstones, creating a captivating contrast of life and death.

2. Moss-Covered Statues: The graves and monuments, many over a century old, are adorned with weathered, moss-covered statues that add to the cemetery's otherworldly charm.

3. A Maze of Tombs: Père Lachaise is a labyrinth of tombs, mausoleums, and crypts. The sheer scale of the cemetery is both breath-taking and overwhelming.

4. Gargoyles and Angels: The sculptures adorning the tombs often include haunting angels, weeping women, and solemn gargoyles, giving the cemetery a gothic quality.

5. Fading Names: Many tombstones and memorials are worn by time, with inscriptions fading into obscurity, adding to the eerie atmosphere.

Père Lachaise Cemetery is a place where the past and present coexist in ethereal harmony, where the famous and the forgotten rest side by side, and where legends continue to captivate the curious. As you explore its haunting beauty, you'll find yourself immersed in a realm where the line between life and death blurs, and where history, art, and eternity unite in solemn splendour.

Chapter 6: Secret Gardens of Paris

Discovering the Hidden Green Oases of the City of Light

Paris, renowned for its iconic landmarks and bustling boulevards, also hides a treasure trove of secret gardens that offer respite from the urban hustle and bustle. In this chapter, we'll uncover the lush and tranquil oases that are the Secret Gardens of Paris. Prepare to wander through the enchanting Parc des Buttes-Chaumont, delve into the botanical beauty of Jardin des Plantes, take a trip around the world in the Albert Kahn Garden, and step into the royal retreat of Parc de Bagatelle.

Parc des Buttes-Chaumont: A Hidden Oasis

Nestled in the 19th arrondissement, the Parc des Buttes-Chaumont is a verdant paradise that provides an escape from the city's bustling streets. This enchanting park offers a tranquil setting, adorned with dramatic cliffs, a shimmering lake, and architectural wonders:

1. Natural Beauty: The park's centrepiece is a serene lake with a central island crowned by the Temple de la Sibylle, a graceful structure reminiscent of ancient Greece. The 63-meter-high cliff known as Belvédère Sybil, offering panoramic views of Paris, adds to the park's allure.

2. Lush Gardens: Parc des Buttes-Chaumont boasts beautifully landscaped gardens, including the Rosary, a delightful collection of roses, and the Bamboo Garden, an oasis of tranquillity.

3. Suspension Bridge: The park is home to a whimsical suspension bridge that leads to the island. Crossing it is an adventure in itself, offering breath-taking vistas of the lake and the surrounding greenery.

4. Romantic Strolls: The park is ideal for romantic walks, picnics, and unwinding amidst nature's splendour. It's a favourite spot for locals seeking a peaceful escape from the city.

5. Outdoor Cinema: During the summer months, the park hosts open-air cinema screenings, allowing you to enjoy classic movies beneath the starry Parisian sky.

Jardin des Plantes: Botanical Beauty

Jardin des Plantes, located in the 5th arrondissement, is a botanical masterpiece that has been captivating visitors for centuries. It houses a stunning collection of plants, along with an array of captivating attractions:

1. The Great Evolution Gallery: This incredible gallery is home to an extensive collection of fossils and prehistoric creatures, providing insight into the evolution of life on Earth.

2. The Alpine Garden: Discover a diverse range of alpine plants and rock gardens that are a treat for botany enthusiasts and nature lovers.

3. The Ménagerie: The Jardin des Plantes also hosts a zoo, the Ménagerie, which is the oldest public zoo in France. Here, you can admire a variety of animals, including big cats, reptiles, and rare species.

4. The Rose Garden: Take a leisurely stroll through the enchanting Rose Garden, which features a multitude of rose varieties in full bloom during the summer months.

5. The Greenhouses: The park also boasts a collection of stunning greenhouses, including the Winter Garden, which houses tropical and subtropical plants, and the Mexican Hothouse, featuring an array of cacti and succulents.

Albert Kahn Garden: A Trip around the World

The Albert Kahn Garden, located in Boulogne-Billancourt, takes you on a globe-trotting journey through meticulously designed gardens that represent various parts of the world:

1. Japanese Garden: Immerse yourself in the tranquillity of the Japanese Garden, featuring traditional elements like a bridge, a tea pavilion, and an authentic tea ceremony.

2. English Garden: Stroll through the picturesque English Garden, a haven of greenery complete with a lovely meandering stream.

3. French Garden: The French Garden displays the elegance of formal French garden design, with meticulously manicured hedges and flowerbeds.

4. Forest of Vosges: Take a walk in the Forest of Vosges, a serene woodland area that offers a taste of the French countryside.

5. The Blue Forest: The mystical Blue Forest, awash in hues of blue and purple, is an enchanting spot for reflection and relaxation.

Parc de Bagatelle: A Royal Retreat

Tucked away in the Bois de Boulogne, Parc de Bagatelle is a hidden gem with a regal history. It offers the perfect blend of French formal gardens, floral displays, and a charming château:

1. Bagatelle Château: The park is home to the stunning Château de Bagatelle, a neoclassical palace surrounded by lush gardens. The château is open for guided tours and is a marvel of architecture.

2. Rose Garden: Parc de Bagatelle is famous for its exquisite rose garden, which boasts over 10,000 rose bushes representing more than 1,200 different species. The annual International Rose Competition held here is a visual spectacle.

3. Japanese Garden: The park also houses a delightful Japanese Garden with a pond, bridges, and a tea house, offering an oasis of serenity within the larger park.

4. The Iris Garden: The park features a mesmerizing Iris Garden with an array of colourful irises that bloom in a breath-taking spectacle during the spring.

5. Temple of Love: Visit the charming Temple of Love, an ornate structure at the heart of the park that offers a romantic ambiance.

Each of these secret gardens reveals a distinct facet of Paris's allure, from the tranquil and dramatic to the enchanting and botanical. They offer a counterbalance to the city's urban energy, inviting you to explore these hidden green oases and create your own moments of tranquillity and contemplation.

Chapter 7: Music and Art beyond Louvre
Unlocking the Creative Pulse of Paris

While the Louvre Museum is renowned for its unparalleled collection of art, Paris has a thriving alternative arts scene that extends far beyond the grand halls of the Louvre. In this chapter, we will delve into the world of alternative art galleries, uncover underground music venues, immerse ourselves in the vibrant street performances and buskers, and explore the artistic communities that thrive outside the shadow of the Louvre.

Exploring Alternative Art Galleries

Paris's artistic landscape is far from limited to the Louvre. The city harbours a multitude of alternative art galleries, where innovative and boundary-pushing works are on display. These galleries are where you can experience the cutting-edge of the art world:

1. Palais de Tokyo: Located across the Seine River from the Eiffel Tower, the Palais de Tokyo is a contemporary art centre that showcases emerging and avant-garde artists. With its ever-changing exhibitions, this space provides a glimpse into the future of art.

2. La Maison Rouge: Nestled in the 12th arrondissement, this private foundation is committed to exhibiting contemporary art. The ever-evolving exhibitions encompass a wide range of mediums, from painting and sculpture to video art.

3. 59 Rivoli: Housed in a former squat, this artist-run space in the heart of Paris offers a dynamic setting for contemporary art. The studios and galleries are constantly evolving, allowing visitors to engage with artists and their creative processes.

4. La Colonie: Part cultural space, part experimental gallery, La Colonie is a hub for artistic expression and socio-political discourse. It hosts exhibitions, performances, and discussions that challenge traditional norms.

5. Centquatre-Paris: Located in the 19th arrondissement, this vast space was once a municipal funeral home. Today, it's a vibrant cultural centre featuring exhibitions, live performances, and a diverse array of artistic experiences.

Underground Music Venues

Paris's music scene extends far beyond the traditional concert halls and opera houses. The city boasts a vibrant underground music scene that caters to a wide range of tastes, from indie and punk to electronic and experimental:

1. La Flèche d'Or: Situated in the 20th arrondissement, this former railway station is now a renowned live music venue. It hosts both local and international acts, making it a hotspot for indie music enthusiasts.

2. Le Caveau des Oubliettes: Descend into the depths of this medieval cellar in the Latin Quarter, where jazz and blues take centre stage. The intimate setting and historic ambiance create a unique musical experience.

3. La Java: This iconic venue in the 10th arrondissement is a legendary spot for electronic music, hosting DJs and live acts. Its diverse line-up ensures there's something for everyone.

4. Le Gibus Club: Located near the Canal Saint-Martin, this versatile venue hosts everything from techno parties to live rock shows. Its dynamic programming keeps the nightlife alive.

5. La Bellevilloise: Found in the eclectic neighbourhood of Ménilmontant, La Bellevilloise is a cultural institution featuring a variety of events, including live music, DJ sets, and art exhibitions.

Street Performances and Buskers

The streets of Paris are not just for strolling; they are stages for impromptu performances, artistic expression, and the sounds of talented buskers. Keep an eye out for these captivating street performances:

1. Place Georges-Pompidou: The square in front of the Centre Pompidou often hosts street performers, from musicians and dancers to living statues. It's a lively place to enjoy spontaneous art.

2. Montmartre: As you ascend the steps of Montmartre, you'll encounter a medley of buskers showcasing their talents, from accordion players to portrait artists.

3. Seine Riverbanks: The picturesque Seine Riverbanks become a gathering place for musicians, poets, and painters. Stroll along the quays and immerse yourself in the creativity.

4. Île de la Cité: In the heart of the city, the square in front of Notre-Dame Cathedral often features street musicians and performers. It's a harmonious backdrop to the cathedral's grandeur.

5. Jardin des Tuileries: The beautiful gardens near the Louvre are not just for leisurely walks; they also host occasional street performances, including classical musicians and contemporary dancers.

Artistic Communities beyond the Louvre

Paris's artistic communities thrive in neighbourhoods that extend well beyond the Louvre's precincts. These areas are teeming with studios, galleries, and creative hubs where artists flourish:

1. Belleville: This neighbourhood in the 20th arrondissement is a burgeoning artistic enclave. Its home to numerous artists' studios and independent galleries, making it a hotspot for contemporary art.

2. Le Marais: Beyond its historic charm, Le Marais is also a hub for the LGBTQ+ community and contemporary art. Explore its many galleries, including Galerie Perrotin, and enjoy the vibrant atmosphere.

3. Pantin: Just outside of Paris, Pantin is a burgeoning cultural district known for its artist workshops and studios. The Pantin - Ateliers d'Artistes is a must-visit for a glimpse into the creative process.

4. La Villette: The Parc de la Villette hosts artistic events and exhibitions throughout the year, making it a lively spot for contemporary art and cultural happenings.

5. 13th arrondissement: This district is known for its street art, with mural-covered buildings and regular art festivals. Explore the Galerie Itinerrance for a deeper dive into the world of urban art.

Paris, with its thriving alternative arts scene, underground music venues, and vibrant street performances, is far more than just the Louvre. As you explore these hidden pockets of creativity and engage with the city's artistic communities, you'll discover a Paris that's alive with the pulse of innovation and expression.

Chapter 8: Little-Known Museums

Unveiling Paris's Hidden Treasures of Art and Curiosities

Paris is a city of endless surprises, and its array of museums extends far beyond the iconic Louvre and Musée d'Orsay. In this chapter, we will uncover the city's little-known museums, where extraordinary collections, bizarre curiosities, and unconventional themes await. Prepare to explore the Musée de la Chasse et de la Nature, venture into the realm of legends at the Museum of Vampires and Legendary Creatures, immerse yourself in the surrealism of the Salvador Dalí Museum, and witness the world of illusion at the Musée de la Magie.

Musée de la Chasse et de la Nature

Tucked away in the heart of the Marais district, the Musée de la Chasse et de la Nature (Museum of Hunting and Nature) offers a unique and captivating experience. This museum delves into the world of hunting and its intricate relationship with nature:

1. Fascinating Artefacts: The museum's collection spans a diverse array of artefacts, from antique firearms and taxidermy animals to intricate hunting gear and period costumes.

2. Unique Exhibits: The Musée de la Chasse et de la Nature is home to some truly unique exhibits, including an impressive display of hunting trophies and a room dedicated to the art of falconry.

3. Surreal Installations: Contemporary art installations add a surreal touch to the museum, making it a thought-provoking space for artists and art enthusiasts.

4. Themed Rooms: The museum features intricately designed themed rooms, such as the Cabinet of Curiosities, where you can explore an eclectic array of natural and man-made curiosities.

5. Historical Insights: The museum offers fascinating insights into the history and evolution of hunting practices and their impact on the natural world.

The Museum of Vampires and Legendary Creatures

For those who dare to explore the world of the supernatural, the Museum of Vampires and Legendary Creatures, located in the heart of Paris, offers a journey into the realm of myths, legends, and all things mysterious:

1. Vampires and beyond: This museum delves into the lore of vampires from different cultures, offering an extensive collection of artefacts, books, and artwork related to these mythical creatures.

2. Myths and Legends: Beyond vampires, the museum explores other legendary beings, such as werewolves, mermaids, and dragons, revealing the universal fascination with the supernatural.

3. Macabre Artefacts: The museum's collection includes eerie and macabre artefacts, from ancient vampire-killing kits to artistic representations of these mysterious beings.

4. Interactive Experience: Visitors have the opportunity to interact with exhibits, making it an engaging and immersive journey into the world of the supernatural.

5. The Occult and the Unknown: The museum also explores the world of the occult, paranormal phenomena, and unexplained mysteries, adding an air of mystery to your visit.

The Salvador Dalí Museum

Nestled in the charming neighbourhood of Montmartre, the Salvador Dalí Museum offers a surreal journey into the mind of one of the 20th century's most renowned artists:

1. The World of Dalí: This museum houses an extensive collection of Salvador Dalí's works, including paintings, sculptures, and drawings, offering a comprehensive view of the artist's creative genius.

2. Surrealism Unleashed: The museum showcases the surrealism movement through Dalí's extraordinary artwork, as well as his eccentric personality and eccentricities.

3. The Mae West Room: One of the highlights is the Mae West Room, an installation that invites visitors to view the world through the eyes of the artist, just as he did when painting his iconic "Face of Mae West."

4. Dalí's Personal Collection: The museum also features a selection of personal items, curiosities, and objects that reveal the man behind the eccentric persona.

5. Artistic Experience: The Salvador Dalí Museum offers an immersive experience that takes you on a surreal journey through the artist's life, work, and fascination with the absurd.

Musée de la Magie: A World of Illusion

Nestled in the historic Marais district, the Musée de la Magie (Museum of Magic) is a hidden gem dedicated to the world of illusion, magic, and prestidigitation:

1. Magical History: The museum provides a captivating insight into the history of magic, with a collection of antique magic props, books, and posters dating back to the 18th century.

2. Enchanting Exhibits: Visitors can witness enchanting exhibits, including optical illusions, automata, and interactive displays that reveal the secrets behind classic magic tricks.

3. Houdini's Chamber: A highlight of the museum is Houdini's Chamber, a recreation of the legendary magician's workshop, filled with his personal belongings and magic memorabilia.

4. Live Magic Shows: The Musée de la Magie offers live magic shows that demonstrate classic tricks and illusions, adding a touch of wonder to your visit.

5. Hidden Library: The museum houses a hidden library filled with rare books on magic, making it a valuable resource for those interested in the art of illusion.

These little-known museums, with their eccentric themes and captivating collections, offer a delightful alternative to the well-trodden paths of Paris's more famous cultural institutions. As you explore these hidden treasures, you'll embark on a journey through the obscure, the surreal, and the magical, uncovering the rich tapestry of curiosities that Paris has to offer.

Chapter 9: Subterranean Paris: Catacombs and Underground Tunnels

Descending into the Depths of Paris's Hidden World

Beneath the romantic avenues and iconic landmarks of Paris lies a shadowy realm of tunnels, quarries, and catacombs. In this chapter, we will delve into the depths of Subterranean Paris, uncovering the eerie history of the catacombs, learning how to visit them responsibly, unveiling the secrets of underground tunnels, and embarking on an adventure to explore the city's hidden depths.

The History of the Catacombs

1. Ancient Quarries: The catacombs of Paris have their origins in the city's extensive network of underground quarries, known as the "Carrières de Paris." These quarries provided the stone that was used to build Paris, including famous structures like Notre-Dame Cathedral.

2. Overcrowded Cemeteries: By the 18th century, Parisian cemeteries had become overcrowded, leading to unsanitary conditions and public health concerns. To address this, city officials decided to relocate the remains of millions of Parisians to the abandoned quarries.

3. Transformation into Ossuary: The catacombs were transformed into an ossuary, and the relocation of bones began in 1786. It took several years to complete, and the result is a chilling but fascinating underground labyrinth of stacked human remains.

4. The Tourist Attraction: In the early 19th century, the catacombs were opened to the public, and they have been a unique and eerie tourist attraction ever since.

How to Visit the Catacombs Responsibly

Visiting the catacombs is a unique and thought-provoking experience, but it should be done with respect for the history and those interred there. Here's how to visit the catacombs responsibly:

1. Be Mindful and Respectful: Remember that the catacombs are not a traditional tourist destination; they are a resting place for the deceased. Maintain a respectful and solemn demeanour while exploring.

2. Follow the Rules: Abide by the rules and guidelines set by the staff during your visit. These rules are in place to ensure both your safety and the preservation of the catacombs.

3. Stay with Your Group: It's easy to get lost in the winding passages, so always stay with your group or guide. Venturing off alone can be dangerous.

4. No touching or Vandalism: Do not touch or disturb the bones, and certainly do not vandalize the catacombs in any way.

5. Respect Photography Rules: Follow any rules regarding photography, which may vary depending on the area you are visiting. Flash photography may not be permitted in some sections.

Secret Underground Tunnels and Stories

The catacombs are just one part of Subterranean Paris. Beneath the streets, an intricate web of tunnels and chambers exists, each with its own history and intrigue:

1. The "Quarries of Paris": The catacombs are only a small portion of the extensive quarry network beneath Paris. Many sections of these quarries are off-limits to the public and are a fascination for urban explorers.

2. Catacomb Explorers: A group of intrepid individuals known as "cataphiles" explore the hidden catacombs, often descending into the labyrinth through secret entrances in the city. They have mapped the catacombs extensively and continue to uncover new sections.

3. Secret Societies: Over the years, various secret societies have used the catacombs for clandestine meetings and rituals. These stories add an air of mystique to the underground world.

4. Lost and Found: The catacombs have a history of lost and found. People have become disoriented in the labyrinthine passages, sometimes spending days underground before being rescued.

5. Mysterious Graffiti: The walls of the catacombs are adorned with graffiti, much of it created by the cataphiles. These artworks tell a story of the subterranean world.

Exploring the City's Hidden Depths

Beyond the catacombs, Subterranean Paris offers a wealth of underground attractions and tunnels to explore:

1. Paris Sewer Museum: The Musée des Égouts de Paris (Paris Sewer Museum) offers a unique look at the city's sewer system. It's a fascinating journey beneath the streets.

2. Hidden Tunnels and Passages: Paris is riddled with hidden tunnels, some of which are off-limits to the public. However, there are guided tours that allow you to explore sections of these intriguing passages.

3. La Petite Ceinture: La Petite Ceinture, or "the little belt," is a disused railway line that encircles Paris. It's become a haven for urban explorers and photographers, offering a glimpse of Paris's forgotten history.

4. The Phantom Metro Stations: Paris has several "phantom" metro stations, closed to the public but occasionally used for filming and special events. Some, like Haxo, are worth seeking out for their unique architecture.

5. Hidden Catacomb Entrances: In some neighbourhoods, you can find unassuming entrances that lead down into the catacombs. These are often used by cataphiles and adventurers.

Subterranean Paris is a realm of history, mystery, and adventure that awaits those willing to venture into its depths. As you explore this hidden world, you'll gain a new perspective on the City of Light and uncover the secrets that lie beneath its bustling streets.

Chapter 10: Beyond the Eiffel Tower: Neighbourhoods along the Seine

Exploring Enchanting Quarters and Seine River Delights

While the Eiffel Tower commands attention, Paris's charm extends far beyond this iconic landmark. In this chapter, we will guide you through the delightful neighbourhoods along the Seine, including the historic Île de la Cité and Île Saint-Louis, the vibrant Latin Quarter, the picturesque Seine riverbanks, and the quest for unconventional views of the Eiffel Tower.

Île de la Cité and Île Saint-Louis

1. The Heart of Paris: The Île de la Cité is the very heart of Paris, where the city was born. Its home to the majestic Notre-Dame Cathedral, a masterpiece of Gothic architecture with its famous flying buttresses and intricate rose windows.

2. Charming Île Saint-Louis: Just a stone's throw from Île de la Cité, you'll find Île Saint-Louis, a peaceful island that feels like a serene village in the heart of the city. Explore its narrow streets, quaint boutiques, and charming cafés.

3. Berthillon Ice Cream: Be sure to savour a scoop of Berthillon ice cream, celebrated as one of the best in the world. The tiny shop on Île Saint-Louis offers a delightful selection of flavours.

4. Hidden Gardens: Discover the secret garden of Square du Vert-Galant, located at the western tip of Île de la Cité. It's an idyllic spot for a leisurely stroll or a romantic picnic.

5. Shakespeare and Company: On the Left Bank, you'll find the famous English-language bookstore, Shakespeare and Company. It's a literary haven that has welcomed writers like Hemingway and Joyce.

Latin Quarter: Student Life and Hidden Gems

1. Student Vibes: The Latin Quarter is named after the Latin language, once the common tongue of universities in the area. Today, it remains a vibrant student hub, home to the Sorbonne and other prestigious institutions.

2. The Panthéon: Don't miss the impressive Panthéon, a neoclassical mausoleum where great French figures like Voltaire and Marie Curie are buried.

3. Rue Mouffetard: Explore the charming Rue Mouffetard, a lively market street lined with cafés, food stalls, and shops. It's a great place for people-watching.

4. Hidden Courtyards: Some of the Latin Quarter's treasures are tucked away in hidden courtyards. Seek out the Cour de Rohan, an elegant space hidden behind an unassuming door.

5. Place de la Contrescarpe: Enjoy the lively atmosphere of Place de la Contrescarpe, a popular square surrounded by cafés and restaurants. It's a great spot to unwind.

The Picturesque Seine River Banks

1. Riverside Strolls: Take leisurely strolls along the picturesque Seine riverbanks, lined with book stalls, street vendors, and street performers. It's a great way to soak in the city's charm.

2. Square du Vert-Galant: We've already mentioned the secret garden on Île de la Cité, but it's worth noting that it offers some of the most stunning views of the Seine and the surrounding architecture.

3. Batobus: For a unique perspective of the Seine, consider a ride on the Batobus, a water bus that allows you to hop on and off at various locations along the river.

4. Seine River Cruises: Several operators offer Seine River cruises, providing a romantic and panoramic view of Paris's iconic landmarks, including the Eiffel Tower and Notre-Dame Cathedral.

5. Institut de France: Admire the elegant façade of the Institut de France, a beautiful neoclassical building that houses several learned societies, including the Académie Française.

Unconventional Views of the Eiffel Tower

1. Parc des Buttes-Chaumont: For a unique vantage point of the Eiffel Tower, head to Parc des Buttes-Chaumont. Climb to the Temple de la Sibylle, an ornate structure that offers breath-taking views of the city.

2. Montparnasse Tower: The Montparnasse Tower, while often overlooked, provides one of the best views of Paris, as it offers a panorama that includes the Eiffel Tower.

3. Passy Cemetery: A peaceful and unconventional spot for viewing the Eiffel Tower is Passy Cemetery, where you can pay your respects to famous figures while enjoying the skyline.

4. Bir-Hakeim Bridge: Stroll across the Bir-Hakeim Bridge, which offers stunning views of the Eiffel Tower framed by its ornate steel arches.

5. Trocadéro Gardens at Sunrise: To see the Eiffel Tower without the crowds, visit the Trocadéro Gardens at sunrise. The soft morning light casts a magical glow on this iconic monument.

These neighbourhoods along the Seine, with their rich history, vibrant life, and unconventional views, allow you to experience a Paris beyond the Eiffel Tower. As you explore their hidden gems and charming corners, you'll discover the intricate tapestry of the city's soul.

Chapter 11: Nightlife in Unexpected Places

Unveiling Paris's Hidden Night-time Delights

Paris is renowned for its world-class restaurants and iconic nightlife districts, but the City of Light also harbours a secret world of after-dark delights in unexpected places. In this chapter, we'll lead you through alternative nightlife venues and events, introduce you to secret speakeasies and hidden bars, guide you to late-night jazz clubs and cabarets, and invite you to dance under the stars by the Seine.

Alternative Nightlife Venues and Events

Paris's alternative nightlife scene offers unique experiences that diverge from the typical nightclub and bar scene. Explore these venues and events that are a bit off the beaten path:

1. Le Comptoir Général: A haven for creativity and cultural exploration, Le Comptoir Général is a quirky bar and event space that combines art, music, and food in a vibrant atmosphere. Each night brings a new adventure, from poetry readings to live music.

2. Wanderlust: Nestled along the Seine, this open-air venue combines a trendy nightclub with a scenic outdoor space. The perfect destination for dancing under the stars, Wanderlust features DJ sets, live performances, and a spectacular view of the city.

3. Nuits Fauves: Located in an industrial space on the outskirts of Paris, Nuits Fauves is a cutting-edge techno club known for its immersive light shows and international DJ line-ups. It's an underground haven for electronic music enthusiasts.

4. Secret Garden Parties: Keep an eye out for secret garden parties that pop up in Paris during the summer months. These impromptu gatherings feature live music, food, and art installations, often in hidden courtyards and parks.

5. Pop-Up Markets: Paris's pop-up markets, such as the Wanderlust Market, combine shopping with entertainment. You can find fashion, artisanal goods, food stalls, and live music in these vibrant settings.

Secret Speakeasies and Hidden Bars

Speakeasies are hidden gems that evoke the spirit of the Roaring Twenties. They offer an intimate and secretive atmosphere perfect for those seeking a unique nightlife experience:

1. Moonshiner: Disguised as a pizzeria, Moonshiner is accessed through a hidden door at the back. Once inside, you'll find an elegant, dimly lit space offering a wide array of craft cocktails.

2. Lavomatic: Behind a laundromat façade, Lavomatic is a speakeasy known for its creative cocktails and eclectic décor. The ambiance is as captivating as the drinks themselves.

3. Candelaria: This taqueria in the front conceals a charming, candlelit cocktail bar in the rear. Candelaria serves a delightful array of unique drinks and classic cocktails.

4. The Little Red Door: As the name suggests, this discreet bar is behind a little red door, which leads to an elegant space with a focus on craft cocktails. It's an intimate and inviting setting.

5. Le Syndicat: Le Syndicat proudly showcases French spirits and ingredients, making it a unique spot for those looking to explore the world of French cocktails. The bar's industrial chic décor sets a distinctive tone.

Late-Night Jazz Clubs and Cabarets

Paris's jazz clubs and cabarets come to life after dark, offering sultry, soulful evenings filled with music, dance, and captivating performances:

1. Le Caveau de la Huchette: Tucked in the Latin Quarter, Le Caveau de la Huchette is a renowned jazz club where you can revel in live jazz and swing music while dancing the night away.

2. Le Duc des Lombards: This intimate jazz club, set in the heart of Paris, features both local and international jazz talent, ensuring a memorable evening of live music.

3. Le Moulin Rouge: The iconic cabaret of Montmartre, Le Moulin Rouge is famous for its extravagant shows, can-can dancers, and sumptuous entertainment that transports you back to the Belle Époque.

4. Le Crazy Horse: Known for its sensual and avant-garde performances, Le Crazy Horse presents a captivating cabaret experience that combines music, dance, and visual art.

5. La Bellevilloise: A cultural space by day, La Bellevilloise transforms into a lively venue for jazz and world music at night. The charming interior and diverse musical offerings make it a hidden gem for music enthusiasts.

Dancing Under the Stars by the Seine

Paris's Seine riverbanks offer a magical backdrop for dancing al fresco. Experience the romance of dancing under the stars with these delightful options:

1. Guinguette-Resto Rosa Bonheur: This open-air venue on the banks of the Seine offers dance nights where you can waltz, tango, or swing

dance to live music. The relaxed atmosphere makes it perfect for a night of outdoor dancing.

2. La Dame de Canton: Aboard a beautifully restored Chinese junk boat, La Dame de Canton offers dance parties with live bands. The combination of music, river views, and open-air dancing is an enchanting experience.

3. La Javelle: La Javelle is a trendy open-air space located along the Seine, where you can enjoy a wide variety of events, including dance parties, live music, and food trucks. It's a vibrant place for dancing and mingling by the river.

4. Rosa Bonheur sur Seine: This charming riverside venue is a great place to enjoy a relaxed evening of dancing, with an eclectic mix of music that draws a lively crowd.

5. L'Alcazar: Overlooking the Seine, L'Alcazar offers a beautiful terrace where you can dance the night away while sipping on craft cocktails and enjoying the breeze from the river.

Paris comes alive at night, and its alternative nightlife venues offer a refreshing departure from the traditional scene. As you explore these hidden gems, secret speakeasies, late-night jazz clubs, and dance spots by the Seine, you'll discover the city's vibrant nocturnal soul.

Chapter 12: Uncovering the Secrets of Street Art

Exploring Paris's Vibrant Urban Canvases and Underground Art Scenes

While Paris is celebrated for its classic art and historic monuments, the city's vibrant street art scene is equally captivating. In this chapter, we'll trace the evolution of street art in Paris, take you on guided street art tours, introduce you to mesmerizing murals, graffiti, and hidden gems, and present you with some of the most renowned Parisian street artists.

The Evolution of Street Art in Paris

1. From the Margins to the Mainstream: Paris's street art scene has come a long way from its countercultural origins. What was once considered vandalism is now embraced as a legitimate art form, with the city government even commissioning public artworks.

2. The Birth of Stencil Art: Paris played a pivotal role in the global rise of stencil art. Artists like Blek le Rat and Jef Aérosol were among the pioneers who transformed the streets into their canvases.

3. Merging of Styles: Parisian street art reflects a fusion of styles, from traditional graffiti to abstract and contemporary art. It's a dynamic playground where artists experiment with different techniques.

4. The Influence of Parisian Life: The streets of Paris inspire artists with the city's history, culture, and the everyday experiences of its inhabitants. You'll find political statements, social commentary, and whimsical art pieces that capture the essence of Paris.

5. Legal and Temporary Installations: Paris offers a canvas for legal and temporary street art installations. Keep an eye out for works commissioned for specific events, festivals, or as part of regeneration projects.

Guided Street Art Tours

1. Le Mur: This ever-changing street art wall, located in the 11th arrondissement, is dedicated to showcasing the works of local and international artists. Each month, a new artist is invited to leave their mark.

2. Belleville Street Art Tour: Explore the lively district of Belleville on a guided street art tour, where you can discover hidden gems, murals, and works by both emerging and established artists.

3. Urban Art Jungle: This tour takes you on a street art journey through the 13th arrondissement, home to the iconic Street Art 13 mural project. You'll encounter numerous large-scale artworks.

4. Paris Street Art Tour: A comprehensive walking tour that introduces you to the city's most renowned street art areas, including the historic Le Marais, Canal Saint-Martin, and Belleville.

5. Montmartre Street Art Tour: Uncover the secrets of Montmartre, not just as a tourist destination but as a vibrant neighbourhood where street artists express their creativity on the city's walls.

Murals, Graffiti, and Hidden Gems

1. Le Mur des Je t'aime: This artistic treasure is located in the Montmartre district. It's a wall adorned with the words "I love you" in over 300 languages, a testament to the universal language of love.

2. Art Azoi: Dive into the Parisian street art scene with Art Azoi, an artistic duo known for their whimsical and colourful creations that brighten the city's walls.

3. Oberkampf Street: The Oberkampf Street in the 11th arrondissement is a hub for street art. Its ever-changing murals and graffiti showcase the vitality of the city's urban art scene.

4. Père-Lachaise Cemetery Art: While exploring the famous Père-Lachaise Cemetery, keep an eye out for hidden works of art, as some gravestones feature unique graffiti and street art.

5. Hidden Murals in Montreuil: Venture into the eastern suburb of Montreuil, where you can discover murals by local and international artists hidden within its labyrinthine streets.

Renowned Parisian Street Artists

1. JR: Known for his large-scale black-and-white portraits pasted on city walls, JR's work often carries social and political messages. He gained international recognition for his "Inside Out" project.

2. Invader: The elusive artist Invader specializes in pixelated mosaic art inspired by early video games. He's left his "space invaders" on walls around the world, including Paris.

3. Miss.Tic: A prominent figure in Paris's street art scene, Miss.Tic combines poetry and art in her stencilled works. Her pieces often feature strong, feminist messages.

4. C215 (Christian Guémy): Renowned for his intricately detailed stencilled portraits, C215's art adorns the streets of Paris and other major cities worldwide.

5. SETH: Street artist SETH is celebrated for his expressive and emotionally charged murals. His work often explores themes of childhood, innocence, and loss.

Paris's streets are an ever-evolving gallery of urban expression, a testament to the creative spirit that pulses through the city. As you explore the city's street art, you'll discover hidden masterpieces, vibrant neighbourhoods, and the legacy of artists who've transformed the ordinary into extraordinary.

Chapter 13: Alternative Paris for Families

Exploring Paris off the Beaten Path with Kids

Paris isn't just for romantic getaways or cultural excursions; it's also a fantastic destination for families. In this chapter, we'll lead you through kid-friendly neighbourhoods and activities, introduce you to off-the-beaten-path family experiences, guide you to educational and unique attractions, and share where to find the best family-friendly food.

Kid-Friendly Neighbourhoods and Activities

1. Le Marais: This historic district is not only charming but also family-friendly. Its narrow streets are perfect for strolling with little ones, and you can explore unique shops, boutiques, and cafés. Don't miss the Musée de la Chasse et de la Nature, a quirky museum that delights children and adults alike.

2. Canal Saint-Martin: Take a leisurely stroll along the picturesque Canal Saint-Martin, where you can watch boats pass through locks and enjoy a relaxed picnic by the water. It's a peaceful escape from the city's hustle and bustle.

3. Parc des Buttes-Chaumont: This hilly park in the 19th arrondissement offers a playground, suspension bridge, and a grotto with a waterfall. It's a fantastic place for kids to run around and explore.

4. Jardin des Plantes: The beautiful Jardin des Plantes not only features extensive gardens but also the Natural History Museum, which houses an impressive collection of fossils and specimens.

5. Cité des Enfants: Located in the Cité des Sciences et de l'Industrie, Cité des Enfants is an interactive science centre where children can engage in hands-on experiments and activities.

Off-the-Beaten-Path Family Experiences

1. Paris Zoological Park: Located in the Vincennes woods, this zoo offers an immersive experience with habitats that mimic the animals' natural environments. It's a hidden gem for animal enthusiasts.

2. Parc Floral de Paris: Escape the crowds at Parc Floral de Paris, a tranquil haven filled with flowers, playgrounds, and even peacocks. It's an ideal spot for a leisurely family picnic.

3. La Petite Ceinture: Explore La Petite Ceinture, a disused railway line that circles Paris. It's a fantastic space for families to go for a walk or bike ride.

4. Musée de la Chasse et de la Nature: Located in Le Marais, this museum is a treasure trove of oddities, featuring exhibits on hunting, taxidermy, and natural history. It's as fascinating as it is quirky.

5. Deyrolle: This unique shop in the 7th arrondissement is part curiosity cabinet, part taxidermy studio, and part curiosity shop. Kids will be captivated by the array of natural specimens.

Educational and Unique Attractions

1. The Catacombs: While the catacombs may seem an unconventional choice for a family outing, older kids with a penchant for history and adventure might find it intriguing. It's a lesson in the city's past.

2. Palais de la Découverte: This science museum offers interactive exhibits and hands-on experiments that can inspire kids to embrace the wonders of the natural world.

3. Musée de la Musique: Explore the Musée de la Musique at the Philharmonie de Paris, where kids can discover a wide range of musical instruments and interactive displays.

4. City of Science and Industry: A paradise for curious minds, this science museum offers exhibits on everything from space exploration to the human body, making learning fun and engaging.

5. Parc Asterix: Located just outside of Paris, Parc Asterix is a theme park based on the beloved French comic series "Asterix." It offers an array of family-friendly rides, live shows, and activities.

Where to Find the Best Family-Friendly Food

1. Le Pain Quotidien: This bakery and café chain is a reliable choice for family meals. They offer a variety of fresh, wholesome foods, including soups, salads, sandwiches, and pastries.

2. L'As du Fallafel: Located in the heart of Le Marais, L'As du Fallafel is renowned for its mouth-watering falafel sandwiches. It's a quick and delicious option for families on the go.

3. Chez L'Ami Jean: This cosy restaurant offers hearty French fare that kids will love, including roast chicken and delicious desserts like profiteroles.

4. Le Marché des Enfants Rouges: This historic covered market in the Marais district features a diverse range of food stalls. It's a great place for a family meal with a variety of options to suit everyone's taste.

5. Creperie Suzette: Treat your family to delectable crepes at Creperie Suzette, where you can choose from both sweet and savoury options. It's a hit with kids and parents alike.

With its diverse neighbourhoods, unique attractions, and an array of family-friendly dining options, Paris is a city that welcomes families with open arms. Exploring alternative Paris with your loved ones will create unforgettable memories and introduce children to the richness of the city's culture and history.

Chapter 14: Practical Tips for Urban Exploration

Mastering the Art of Discovery in the City of Light

Urban exploration in Paris offers a treasure trove of experiences, but it comes with its own set of challenges. In this chapter, we'll equip you with practical tips to navigate the Parisian public transportation system, ensure your safety during urban exploration, connect with local urban exploration communities, and practice sustainable and responsible exploration.

Navigating the Parisian Public Transportation System

1. Metro: The Paris Metro is a convenient and cost-effective way to get around the city. Be sure to purchase a Navigo card for unlimited rides within your chosen zones, or buy single tickets and carnets (packs of 10) at the ticket machines.

2. RER: The RER (Réseau Express Régional) is the suburban rail network that connects the city to the suburbs. It's ideal for exploring areas outside the city centre, such as the Palace of Versailles or Disneyland Paris.

3. Bus: Paris's bus system is extensive and can take you to less touristy areas of the city. Consider using buses for a more relaxed journey with scenic views.

4. Trams: Tramway lines offer another way to explore Paris, connecting various neighbourhoods. They are also excellent for accessing parts of the city not well served by the Metro.

5. Boats: Paris is known for its beautiful Seine River, and boat cruises offer an alternative perspective of the city. Consider taking a Seine River cruise or using the Batobus water bus to access key landmarks.

6. Biking: Paris has embraced biking with its Vélib' system, offering bikes for rent at numerous locations. It's a fun and eco-friendly way to explore the city.

7. Walk: Paris is a pedestrian-friendly city, and walking allows you to soak in its charm and discover hidden gems. Wear comfortable shoes, as you'll be doing a lot of walking.

8. Digital Apps: Download navigation apps like Google Maps or Citymapper, which are valuable tools for getting around Paris and the public transportation system.

9. Off-Peak Hours: Try to use public transportation during off-peak hours to avoid the crowds. Early mornings and late evenings are often more tranquil times to explore.

10. Validate Your Tickets: Ensure you validate your tickets at the beginning of your journey by using the machines provided. Failure to do so can result in fines.

Safety Precautions for Urban Exploration

1. Know the Area: Before embarking on urban exploration, research the area thoroughly, understand its history, and be aware of any potential safety concerns.

2. Travel Light: Only bring essentials. Leave valuables and unnecessary items at home. A lightweight backpack is ideal for carrying water, snacks, and other necessities.

3. Let Someone Know: Always inform someone you trust about your exploration plans, including the location and expected duration of your adventure.

4. Stay Aware: Be alert to your surroundings, and trust your instincts. If a location feels unsafe, it's best to leave.

5. Dress appropriately: Wear comfortable clothing and appropriate footwear. Bring layers, as some locations may be dark, damp, or cold.

6. Respect Private Property: Avoid trespassing on private property. Seek permission when needed, and adhere to any posted signs or warnings.

7. Carry Essentials: Carry a flashlight, first aid kit, and a charged phone. It's also a good idea to have a power bank and a map of the area.

8. Be Cautious of Hazards: Watch for uneven terrain, sharp objects, or unstable structures. Stay away from any locations that may pose physical risks.

9. Group Exploration: If you're new to urban exploration, consider going with a group or experienced individuals. Safety in numbers is often a wise choice.

10. Check the Weather: Weather conditions can affect your exploration. Ensure you're prepared for rain, cold, or heat as necessary.

Connecting with Local Urban Exploration Communities

1. Online Forums and Social Media: Join urban exploration forums and groups online to connect with like-minded individuals. Websites like urbexfrance.fr are valuable resources.

2. Local Meetups: Attend local urban exploration meetups, which are organized by various online communities. This is an excellent way to learn from experienced explorers.

3. Use Caution: While building connections, exercise caution and be wary of sharing personal information online or meeting strangers alone.

4. Learn and Share: The urban exploration community is all about learning and sharing. Share your discoveries and respect the work of others.

5. Be a Responsible Explorer: Always prioritize safety, preservation, and respect for the locations you visit. Leave nothing behind but footprints.

Sustainable and Responsible Exploration

1. Leave No Trace: Abide by the "Leave No Trace" principle. Don't litter, vandalize, or damage locations. Respect the environment and historical significance of the sites.

2. Capture Memories, Not Objects: Take photographs and create memories, but refrain from taking souvenirs or disturbing the locations.

3. Follow Local Laws and Regulations: Respect any rules or regulations that apply to specific locations, and adhere to any "No Trespassing" signs.

4. Report Vandalism: If you come across vandalism or damage caused by others, consider reporting it to local authorities or preservation groups.

5. Educate yourself: Learn about the history and cultural significance of the sites you explore. This enriches your experience and promotes respect for the past.

Paris offers a plethora of exciting urban exploration opportunities. With these practical tips, you can navigate the city, ensure your safety, connect with local communities, and explore responsibly. Urban exploration in

Paris will not only satisfy your curiosity but also leave you with lasting memories of this enchanting city.

Don't miss out!

Visit the website below and you can sign up to receive emails whenever PA BOOKS publishes a new book. There's no charge and no obligation.

https://books2read.com/r/B-A-STTAB-XSZPC

BOOKS2READ

Connecting independent readers to independent writers.

Also by PA BOOKS

Hogan's Key
Kimberly & the Five Strange Goldfishes
The Enchanted Library
The Misadventures of Pirate Pete
From Wheel To Web: 40 Remarkable Inventions
Once Upon A Sleepy Time
The Global Game - The Evolution Of Football
Strides To Success: A Beginner's Guide to Running
The ChatGPT Handbook
Climate Crossroads
1000 Everyday Life Hacks
Urban Exploration - London The Comprehensive Travel Guide
Urban Exploration - New York The Comprehensive Travel Guide
Urban Exploration - Amsterdam The Comprehensive Travel Guide
Urban Exploration - Barcelona The Comprehensive Travel Guide
Urban Exploration - Dubai The Comprehensive Travel Guide
Urban Exploration - Paris The Comprehensive Travel Guide